ideals®

THANKSGIVING

Vol. 49, No. 7

Publisher, Patricia A. Pingry
Editor, D. Fran Morley
Art Director, Patrick McRae
Copy Editor, Tim Hamling
Contributing Editors, Lansing Christman,
Deana Deck, Russ Flint, Pamela Kennedy,
John Slobodnik, Nancy J. Skarmeas

ISBN 0-8249-1103-2

IDEALS—Vol. 49, No. 7 November MCMXCII IDEALS
(ISSN 0019-137X) is published eight times a year: Febru-
ary, March, May, June, August, September, November,
December by IDEALS PUBLISHING CORPORATION,
P.O. Box 148000, Nashville, Tenn. 37214. Second-class
postage paid at Nashville, Tennessee, and additional
mailing offices. Copyright © MCMXCII by IDEALS PUB-
LISHING CORPORATION. POSTMASTER: Send
address changes to Ideals, Post Office Box 148000,
Nashville, Tenn. 37214-8000. All rights reserved. Title
IDEALS registered U.S. Patent Office.

SINGLE ISSUE—$4.95
ONE-YEAR SUBSCRIPTION—eight consecutive issues as
published—$19.95
TWO-YEAR SUBSCRIPTION—sixteen consecutive issues
as published—$35.95
Outside U.S.A., add $6.00 per subscription year for postage
and handling.

ACKNOWLEDGMENTS

AUTUMN EVENINGS by Edgar A. Guest from *WHEN
DAY IS DONE*, copyright ©1921 by The Reilly and Lee
Co. Used by permission of the author's estate.
THANKFUL FOR WHAT from *MY KITCHEN WINDOW* by
Edna Jaques, copyright © in Canada by Thomas Allen &
Son Limited. A FAMILY GRACE—THANKSGIVING
DINNER from the book *THE PRAYERS OF PETER
MARSHALL*, compiled and edited by Catherine Marshall,
copyright © 1949, 1950, 1951, 1954, by Catherine
Marshall. Renewed 1982. Published by Chosen Books,
Fleming H. Revell Company. Used by Permission. Our
Sincere Thanks to the following authors whom we were
unable to contact: Margaretta Brown for AUTUMN; Dora
Dickson McBroom for FALLEN LEAVES; Virginia K. Oliver
for BLESSING; Bertha M. Russell for BESIDE A HAR-
VEST FIELD; Myrtella Southerland for ALL THE WORLD
A-GLORY; Richie A. Tankersley for THIS IS
THANKSGIVING; and May Smith White for AUTUMN'S
MYSTERIOUS PATTERN.

Four-color separations by Rayson Films, Inc.,
Waukesha, Wisconsin

Printing by The Banta Company, Menasha, Wisconsin

The paper used in this publication meets the minimum
requirements of American National Standard for Infor-
mation Sciences—Permanence of Paper for Printed
Library Materials, ANSI Z39.48-1984.

Printed on 60# Hi-Bright Recycled Stock

Unsolicited manuscripts will not be returned
without a self-addressed stamped envelope.

Inside Front Cover
Frances Hook

Cover Photo
H. Abernathy   Inside Back Cover
H. Armstrong Roberts, Inc.   John Walter

Autumn's Mysterious Pattern

May Smith White

The day grew quiet here . . . no ripples played
Upon the austere sky. And golden leaves
Hung motionless, as if each one obeyed
The pattern set when browning autumn grieves.
But soon each leaf will yield itself to earth,
Weaving a russet carpet once again—
And autumn fires will then come into birth . . .
Quenched later by the cold November rain.

Here lie the mysteries that autumn keeps;
And through this time, her songs will lull the heart
While plans grow richer, as all nature sleeps,
Because her deftness is her counterpart.
With changing seasons, I still yearn to see
The sign of autumn in the maple tree!

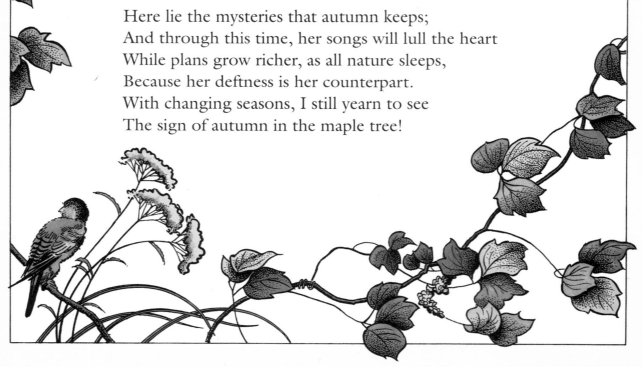

Photo Opposite
MAPLE AND BLUE SPRUCE
Minnesota
Firth Photobank

Autumn

Margaretta Brown

Before our twilight hour descends,
We should portray to all
The beauty of a well-spent life,
As trees do in the fall.

Let crimson leaves be deeds of love;
And leaves of sunset gold
Be friendships made throughout the years,
Whose value is untold.

Let autumn rains be tears we shed
With others in great need,
That kindled hope and renewed faith
May be the fertile seed

Which springs anew in storm-tossed lives
So they in strength may grow;
Then the memory of our lives will be
As a sunset's afterglow.

SWIFTWATER BRIDGE
Swiftwater, New Hampshire
Dick Dietrich Photography

ALL
THE WORLD
A-GLORY

Myrtella Southerland

Once again, November in its beauty,
Scarlet leaves and gold along the lane
Where the maples lure us with their color,
All the world a-glory once again.

RUSTIC FENCE AND FALL COLORS
Brown County State Park, Indiana
Adam Jones Photography

Crimson ivy clinging to the fences,
Late birds singing by the riverside,
Goldenrod and asters yet in blossom,
Olden dreams with mellow eventide.

Bonfires gaily blazing in the twilight.
Kiddies laughing, dancing in their fun,
Cracking nuts they've gathered from the woodland—
What a world, when all is said and done.

Time to gather round the grate-fire, smiling,
Time to put our doubts and fears to rest,
Just to live and love in bright November,
And the glorious world at its best!

INDIAN SUMMER

John Greenleaf Whittier

From gold to gray
Our mild, sweet day
Of Indian summer fades too soon;
But tenderly
Above the sea
Hangs, white and calm, the hunter's moon.

In its pale fire
The village spire
Shows like the zodiac's spectral lance;
The painted walls
Whereon it falls
Transfigured stand in marble trance.

FALLEN LEAVES

Dora Dickson McBroom

I strolled o'er wooded, wind-swept hills
Among bare and naked trees,
And walked, as in loose, drifted snow,
Through brown, soft, rustling leaves.

I felt a wee bit sad at heart,
I missed the colors gay
Of autumn leaves upon the trees
When last I passed this way.

Now, all those gorgeous colored leaves
Lie scattered on the ground;
Few hints of previous wondrous tints
On any can be found.

They're caught by every passing breeze
And circled high in air,
To fall again and huddle close
At the feet of trees so bare.

And thus, dear leaves, your mission fill;
As much your part to be
A shelter for all tender roots,
As swaying high in tree.

Soon, floating low, some soft, grey clouds
Will send a cover warm
Of snowflakes, light as down itself,
To shield you from the storms.

Then, when the springtime comes again
And cold winds disappear,
All leaves and flowers will lovelier be
Because of you, my dears.

Photo Opposite
FALLEN LEAVES
Chiricahua Mountain, Arizona
Willard Clay
FPG International

November
Minnie Klemme

November marks the falling leaves,
The fodder cut and bound in sheaves,
The acorns falling to the ground,
Pheasants making "caution" sounds,
A hunter's moon across the sky,
And wild geese up flying high,

The squirrels in the leafy towers,
All snug against November showers,
When rain turns sleet and sleet turns snow—
That is the way the seasons go.
With winter weather on the way,
There still remains Thanksgiving Day.

November saves the best till last,
It is our nation's famed repast,
And fields and woods and leaf and tree
All join in the festivity.

SUGAR MAPLES
Northern Michigan
Larry West
FPG International

Photo Overleaf
FALL PATHWAY
Baltic, Ohio
Fred Sieb Photography

FALL LEAVES
Jeffry Myers
FPG International

Leaves
Before the Wind

Ernest Jack Sharpe

Little brown leaves scampering before the wind,
Oft' I wonder what you'll be
at your journey's end.

FROST ON LEAVES
Beartooth Mountains, Montana
George Robbins Photography

A coverlet for violets, or other woodland flower?
Guarding them through winter's sleep
   within their forest bower?

Or will you help to form a nest for little creatures wild,
To protect them from the bitter cold
   when snows are deeply piled?

Joyously you scamper before the autumn wind.
Impatient little travelers
   seeking journey's end.

Country CHRONICLE
Lansing Christman

Barns and houses are indicative of God's providence in this month of November. I like to putter around the barn when the mow is filled with hay and the bins are filled with grain, oats, and corn. I like to reflect on the well-stocked cellar of the house, filled with fruits and vegetables sufficient for the cold winter months ahead.

Another thing I enjoy in this season of Thanksgiving is to take long walks when the days are bright and clear. I have noticed, here in the foothills of the Blue Ridge Mountains, that when there has not yet been a killing frost there is evidence that Nature is preparing for the winter months as well.

I was delighted on one such walk when I noticed huge beds of wild morning glories still in bloom, rich and beautiful, in the old fields. There they were, spreading out over the ground, climbing fencerows and old brush piles. A terrace of weeds and dried grasses literally blossomed in hues of red and white, blue, pink, and purple. Some of the deep purple blooms appeared as soft as velvet as they shone in the morning sun.

As a boy, I found special pleasure in the morning glory. My mother always grew them along posts in the yard or a trellis near the veranda. I would sometimes pluck a bloom, close the petals between my fingers, put the stem of the funnel-shaped flower between my lips, and blow. The blossom would swell like a balloon until it finally burst with a soft, gentle pop. As a man, I have preferred to let the morning glories go their way, untouched and unharmed. I prefer they decorate a trellis, or spread their loveliness in the old fields and along the brush rows.

On my walk, I could not help but remember what Doctor Bryan Crenshaw, a retired Methodist minister, once wrote in his column in the local newspaper. He spoke of the beauties of the Carolinas, especially in the fall, and concluded: "Do not let this pass unnoticed. 'A poor world this, if full of care, we have no time to stop and stare.' Take time! Enjoy! And be thankful."

And I am thankful that Nature in all its wisdom has taken the time to store some of summer's beauty for the winter months ahead. Just as a well-stocked cellar and barn will feed the body through the coming months of cold and snow, the provisions of Nature, as seen in the simple morning glory, will feed the soul.

The author of two published books, Lansing Christman has been contributing to Ideals *for almost twenty years. Mr. Christman has also been published in several American, foreign, and braille anthologies. He lives in rural South Carolina.*

Harvest Fields

Mary Howitt

When on the breath of autumn's breeze
    From pastures dry and brown,
Goes floating, like an idle thought,
    The fair, white, thistle-down,
Oh, then what joy to walk at will
Upon the golden harvest-hill.

What joy in dreaming ease to lie
    Amid a field, new-shorn;
And see all 'round on sunlit slopes
    The piled-up shocks of corn;
And send the fancy wandering o'er
All pleasant harvest fields of yore.

I feel the day: I see the field,
    The quivering of the leaves;
The harvest hands from row to row
    Binding the yellow sheaves.
And at this very hour, I know
The bounty of so long ago.

Oh, golden fields of bending corn,
    How beautiful they seem.
The reaper-folk, the piled-up sheaves,
    To me are like a dream;
The sunshine and the very air
Seem like old times and take me there.

Beside a Harvest Field

Bertha M. Russell

I would not ask a holier place than this for prayer.
Here by this harvest field I stand, with my head bare,
And gaze through rows of corn shocks stretching on for miles,
Beholding in them majesty not found in cloistered aisles.

I scan the lengthy furrowed turf where plowmen's feet have trod,
And close beside their steps, I see the footprints of my God.
My heart is rapt with inner joy that I can scarce contain,
As from a distant field I hear the harvesters' refrain.

I cannot join their harvest song; my lips are sealed with awe
Lest I by faltering note should mar their praises of God's law;
Their praises of the truth concealed in grain that fell to earth
To lose itself and come again as something given birth,

To grow in blade and sturdy stem and then in ripened ear—
Who would not stand in silent awe and worship here?
I would not seek a holier place than this to pray;
I here forever would remain were that God's way.

But He who brought the harvest to this golden field
Has many garners to be filled with His rich yield.
I haste away, for human hearts await the truth I've found
As I have here communed with Him on holy ground.

Apple Song

Frances Frost

The apples are seasoned
And ripe and sound.
Gently they fall
On the yellow ground.

The apples are stored
In the dusky bin
Where hardly a glimmer
Of light creeps in.

In the firelit winter
Nights they'll be
The clear, sweet taste
Of a summer tree!

Photo Opposite
JONATHAN APPLES
H. Abernathy
H. Armstrong Roberts, Inc.

Harvest

Gertrude Ryder Bennett

He spoke of harvest, pointed to the field
Where shocks of corn stood boldly in the sun.
The earth was kind to give such lavish yield.
Against the barn were pumpkins piled, each one
A golden promise. Peppers strung and dried
Were red as flame. He took a farmer's pride

In heavy apple trees. He knew the soil.
How well it paid him for a summer's toil!

He spoke of harvest time. She smiled, and yet
She hardly heard him. She was gazing where
The children played, a frolicking quartet
Of curls and rompers, and a grateful prayer
Came to her heart. She saw the meaning of
The harvest, felt the strength of boundless love,
Of answered faith. Four children hard at play—
She smiled and brushed a happy tear away.

Merry Autumn Days

Charles Dickens

'Tis pleasant on a fine spring morn
   To see the buds expand,
'Tis pleasant in the summer time
   To see the fruitful land;
'Tis pleasant on a winter's night
   To sit around the blaze,
But what are joys like these, my boys,
   To merry autumn days!

We hail the merry autumn days,
   When leaves are turning red,
Because they're far more beautiful
   Than anyone has said;
We hail the merry harvest time,
   The gayest of the year;
The time of rich and bounteous crops,
   Rejoicing and good cheer.

FALL HARVEST DISPLAY
Massachusetts
Dianne Dietrich Leis Photography

FROM MY G·A·R·D·E·N JOURNAL

Deana Deck

Begonias

I am mad for cut flowers. When they are in season, the house is a riot of color with pots and jars and baskets and kettles filled to overflowing with bright blossoms. In the fall, however, when the frost begins to nip at flowers in my garden, I call in the emergency team—the African violets and the begonias.

Both are grand when it comes to adding splashes of color to an otherwise drab, winter interior, but to me, the African violet's bloom is too soft and velvety, too spring-like, for a holiday display. Begonias, on the other hand, make perfect holiday plants.

The crisp look of the wax begonia leaf and the brilliance of its color, whether bright green or rich bronze, bring an air of freshness to closed-in winter rooms. The pinks and oranges and reds of the blooms are outstanding as holiday decor. Depending on when frost comes to your area, November may be the perfect time to bring begonias in for the fall.

For many years, it never occurred to me that begonias could become winter house plants. I set out little pots of begonias in convenient corners of the garden and enjoyed them all summer but just ignored them as winter approached. One year, impressed by the fullness and cheerful appearance of a healthy pink wax begonia, I decided to dig it out and bring it indoors in the hopes that I could prolong its blooming past the frost date.

I potted it in a plastic tub which I then settled down into an antique crock and placed under a kitchen window. To my surprise, it bloomed incessantly all winter long with bright, pink blossoms, and I was hopelessly smitten. The following spring, I set it out on the porch, and it continued to bloom throughout the season.

The next fall, I brought in a few more begonias. To offset the gloom of shorter days, I placed two of the white, double-blossomed varieties into red baskets and rotated them between the windowsill and the coffee table all winter. They loved it. For a Thanksgiving centerpiece, I set a small, potted, orange-blooming plant with variegated leaves into a hand-thrown-pottery bowl and surrounded it with colorful sugar maple leaves. From that season on, begonias have been an important and colorful part of all my indoor gardening.

If you don't have garden begonias to move into the house this season, check with friends. Begonias are very easy to propagate; perhaps one of your friends will allow you to snip off a few leaves to start a plant of your own. Dip the stems into a little rooting powder and insert them into sand, a mixture of sand and peat moss, or vermiculite. Keep the potting mixture evenly moist but not soggy. Keep the plants at a temperature of 70° to 75°, and the leaves should root in two to three weeks. This process also works when a favorite plant seems to be getting worn out. The nice thing about propagating begonias in this manner is there will be no surprises. All plants grown from a begonia leaf will look exactly like the parent.

Begonias are easy to care for but will benefit from occasional special care. Snip off fading blossoms to keep the plant looking fresh. The plant can quickly take on a worn, bedraggled look if new blossoms have to fight their way through a mass of drying, old flowerheads. If the plant tends to get leggy, move it into better light and pinch back new stem tips to encourage a bushier appearance. Feed the plants in the spring, midsummer, and early fall with a commercial fertilizer for blooming plants. Keep the soil evenly moist and mist the plants in the winter if your home is especially dry. With this extra care, you will be ensured a pot of bright, blooming begonias all winter long.

Now, when the season for fresh-cut garden flowers begins to wane, you can still have a house full of colorful, bright blossoms just by moving your begonias indoors for the winter.

Deana Deck lives in Nashville, Tennessee, where her garden column is a regular feature in The Tennessean.

Readers'

Treasures from God

I love to feel the warmth
Of a sunbeam passing by;
I like to see the blue that spreads
Across the morning sky.

I'm glad God gave us treasures
To enrich the souls of men.
And the only price we pay for these
Is a "Thank you" now and then.

Rosalie Crane
Everett, Washington

Grateful

We're grateful for the right to live;
    With humble hearts our thanks we give
For all that God in wise mercy sends,
    For health and home, children, friends,

For comfort when we are in need,
    For many a kind and helpful deed,
For happy thoughts and holy talk,
    For His guidance in our daily walk.

Our blessings are many, His praises we'll sing—
Our thanks be to God for everything!

Harriett Womack
Gardena, California

Editor's Note:

Readers are invited to submit unpublished, original poetry for possible publication in future issues of *Ideals*. Please send copies only; manuscripts will not be returned. Writers receive $10 for each published submission. Send material to: "Readers' Reflections," Ideals Publishing Corporation, P.O. Box 140300, Nashville, Tennessee 37214-0300.

Reflections

To Love the Giver

There is so much to be thankful for:
The world and all its charm.
To concentrate on things of life
Would seemingly do no harm.

Yet more important than the things of life,
Our experiences everyday:
The gifts of love, good health, and friends
Are more precious, wouldn't you say?

And above all else comes God,
The Giver of all good things.
We kneel in prayer and send our thanks
For gifts that His love brings.

To Him, be all the power and glory,
For His kingdom will always prevail.
And to you, my friend, be peace on earth,
Good will, and joy without fail.

Together let us praise His Name,
And thank Him for His love.
The greatest of all the gifts we possess
Through His Son, sent from above.

Father Dick Brunskill
Colfax, Illinois

I'm Thankful

The butterfly on painted wings,
The bluebird at my door that sings,

The rain that falls, the winds that blow,
The wheat, the corn, the flowers that grow,

The sun that shines from up above,
The warmth that fills my heart with love,

The trees that stand so green and tall—
I'm thankful, Lord. I love it all!

Rita M. Wiltfang
Sanger, California

33

Thanksgiving

Rev. Samuel Francis Smith

While all creation sings for joy,
Let thoughts of praise our hearts employ
Amid the harmony around,
Let not our tongues be silent found—
    Our music still!

Ten thousand songs of praise we owe
To Him whose glories round us flow,
To Him who bids our sorrows cease

And fills our souls with sacred peace—
   So great His love!

He guides our steps to living streams;
He leads our thoughts to holy themes;
Our wandering feet His love redeems;
By day He cheers us with His light
And gives us sweet repose at night—
   So rich His grace!

Let all who dwell below the sky
Join in the angels' minstrelsy,
Till earth no more is dark with sin,
And heavenly joys their course begin—
   No more to cease!

Thanksgiving Prayer

Kay Hoffman

Lord, let my thanks not be confined
To just one day a year
When friends and family gather round
To share Thanksgiving cheer.

Thou heapest blessings round my door
Each day that dawns anew;
It's only fitting that I kneel
And give my thanks to you.

For shelter warm and ample food,
For family ties held dear,
For love that makes a house a home,
And friendship ever near,

For all the beauty of the earth
In sky, on sea, or land,
For seed time and for harvest,
Rich bounty from thy hand.

It matters not the hour or day,
The season of the year,
Everywhere I look, dear Lord,
Your blessings do appear.

Seated at the festive table,
I bow and humbly pray:
Give me a heart that overflows
With "thanks-living" everyday.

Photo Opposite
PEACEFUL REFLECTIONS
Cold Spring Harbor, New York
Fred Sieb Photography

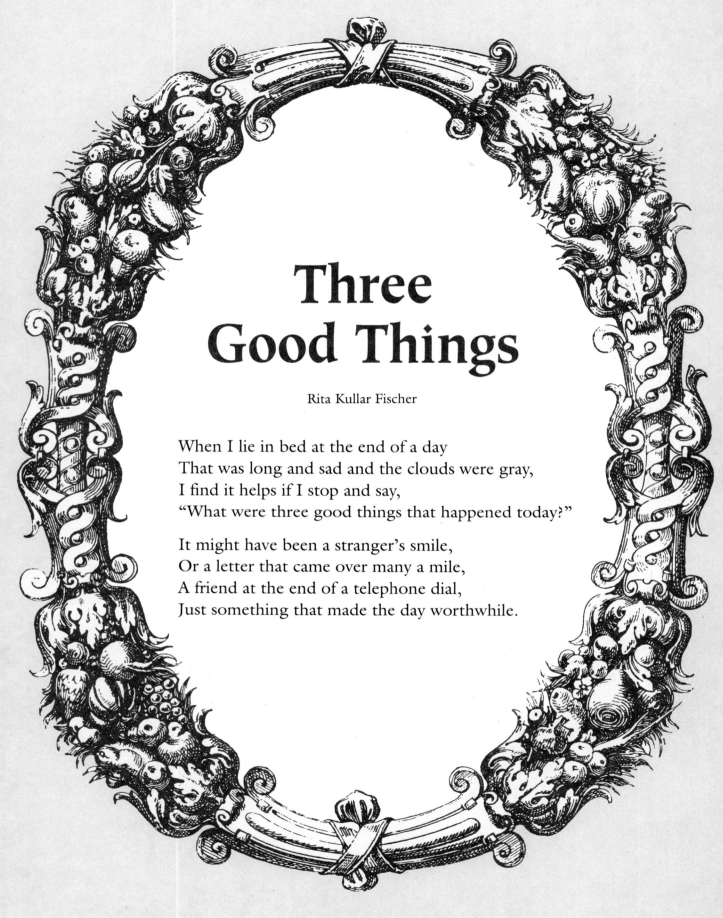

Three Good Things

Rita Kullar Fischer

When I lie in bed at the end of a day
That was long and sad and the clouds were gray,
I find it helps if I stop and say,
"What were three good things that happened today?"

It might have been a stranger's smile,
Or a letter that came over many a mile,
A friend at the end of a telephone dial,
Just something that made the day worthwhile.

It could be a bargain I chanced to buy,
A craft or hobby I'm going to try,
A book that could make me laugh or cry,
A poem or story that made time fly.

It may be the maples touched with gold,
A hummingbird where the sweetpeas grow,
An orange sunset with the mountains below,
The sound of rain, or the water's flow.

It might be a memory from the past,
Some special face that I thought would last,
Or a mountain meadow so wide and vast,
Or a kindness done when I needed one, fast.

No matter how bad my day may be,
How rough the road, how wide the sea,
I thank my God on bended knee
For three good things that happened to me.

Let the Nations Be Glad

from Psalm 67

God be merciful unto us, and bless us;
And cause his face to shine upon us. . . .
That thy way may be known upon earth,
Thy saving health among all nations.
Let the people praise thee, O God;
Let all the people praise thee.

O let the nations be glad and sing for joy:
For thou shalt judge the people righteously,
And govern the nations upon earth.
Let the people praise thee, O God;
Let all the people praise thee.
Then shall the earth yield her increase;
And God, even our own God, shall bless us.

BITS & PIECES

God's goodness hath been great to thee. Let never day nor night unhallowed pass but still remember what the Lord hath done.

From *Henry VI*
William Shakespeare

The worship most acceptable to God comes from a thankful and cheerful heart.

Plutarch

From David learn to give thanks for everything. Every furrow in the Book of Psalms is sown with the seeds of thanksgiving.

Jeremy Taylor

So once in every year we throng
    Upon a day apart,
To praise the Lord with feast and song
    In thankfulness of heart.

Arthur Guiterman

Let my voice ring out and over the earth,
    Through all the grief and strife,
With a golden joy in a silver mirth:
    Thank God for life.

James Thomson

Heap high the board with plenteous
    cheer and gather to the feast,
And toast the sturdy Pilgrim band
    whose courage never ceased.
Give praise to that All-Gracious One
    By whom their steps were led,
And thanks unto the harvest's Lord
    who sends our "daily bread."

Alice Williams Brotherton

A grateful thought toward heaven is of itself a prayer.

Gotthold E. Lessing

If gratitude is due from children to their earthly parent, how much more is the gratitude of the great family of men due to our father in heaven.

Hosea Ballou

Best of all is it to preserve everything in a pure, still heart, and let there be for every pulse a thanksgiving, and for every breath a song.

Konrad von Gesner

What could now sustain them but the spirit of God and his grace? May not and ought not the children of these fathers rightly say: "Our fathers were Englishmen which came over this great ocean and were ready to perish in this wilderness; but they cried unto the Lord, and he heard their voice. . . . Let them therefore praise the Lord because he is good and his mercies endure forever. . . ."

William Bradford

Photo Overleaf
LANDING OF THE PILGRIM FATHERS
from a lithograph by Currier and Ives

THROUGH MY WINDOW

Pamela Kennedy

A *Mayflower* Journal

Day 1: Papa and Mama said I must keep a journal of this journey across the Atlantic. Someday, they say, my children might like to know how it was that their mother left England to come to the New World. I would first like them to know that I did not wish to come. It is a hard thing to leave my friends and dear Grandmama and her gray cat Miranda and the happy times in the garden. My brother Samuel thinks it is "great adventure" to sail across the sea. But already I long for home.

Day 5: The ship at first appeared so large and sturdy, but upon the sea it seems very small. I am fearful it will break apart and we shall all sink to a watery grave! When the wind and waves beat at the hull, my heart pounds, and I cling to the coverlets on the bunks we share. Samuel mocks me and calls me a scared-cat, but I think he is frightened too. Mama says we must pray, but I wonder if God can see such a small ship on such a large ocean.

Day 20: I do try to be a good daughter and not complain, but the food is so awful. The meat is salty, and the biscuits are hard as bricks. It is the same day after day. Mama has tried to keep us contented by telling us stories and singing songs. Yesterday she told us of Jonah from the Bible, and Samuel said he'd like to catch that big fish so we might have a proper meal! I laughed, but Mama said it is not proper to make a joke of God's word.

Day 25: Elder Brewster has established a school. He has many books and is most generous about letting us borrow them. After I have done my lessons and if it is not stormy, I sometimes take one of the books up on the deck and find a "nest" among the ropes and canvas. There, I can be alone and away from the dark and smelly hold. When I am lost in these dear friends—as I have come to call my books—I can forget my hunger and loneliness. It is one of the few joys here aboard *Mayflower*.

Day 30: It has been a month since we left England, but it seems like years! Constanta Hopkins, who is 11, same as I, is now my good friend. We sometimes play at house, pretending we are mamas to the little children on board. I have decided that if I ever do get married and have children, I shall never, never take them on a sea voyage.

Day 40: I think there is quite a bit of quarreling going on among the grown-ups. When they think we cannot hear them, they argue. Many think we should turn back. I heard one man say we are off course and the Captain has no idea where we are! Others think we must pray more and continue. I did not want to come on this journey, but now, I do hope we continue.

Day 45: Yesterday a most amazing thing happened. Master John Howland had gone up on the deck for some air, and just as he took his first step, the ship pitched, and he was thrown in to the sea. As he fell into the sea, he caught hold of the halyards. There was shouting and running, and several sailors hauled poor half-drowned Master Howland back aboard. Now Mama and Papa are so frightened about us falling overboard; we must spend even more time below the deck. It is wet here all the time and cold as well.

Day 50: There are many people who are very sick now. Papa says it is the scurvy and that there is no cure but prayer and the sight of land. The water washes down upon us and tastes like tears. I am truly fearful. My mama does not look well, and Constanta's mama is feeling poorly too. She is going to have a baby, but surely she will wait until we reach our new home.

Day 63: Something very wonderful has happened. Constanta's mama had a baby boy. They have named him Oceanus because he was born on the sea. I was able to hold him for a few moments, and it was a solemn thing to look at how tiny and perfect he is. I think perhaps God does see the little things after all. This baby boy has given us all new hope, and people are more cheerful this week.

Day 64: Today the air seemed different. Samuel told us that he had seen some driftwood in the water. Constanta and I begged Mama to take us upon deck so we could see for ourselves. The water was calmer, and we saw sea birds flying in the sky. The sailors said this means land is nearby. We looked all day long but saw no land. Everyone seems more hopeful.

Day 65: Today, Friday, November 10, 1620, is a day I shall always remember. Early in the morning we heard the call we have waited over two months for—"Land Ho!" Everyone dashed up on the deck at the same time. The land was just a long, gray line on the horizon. It is strange to think of it as home, but I am glad I have Mama and Papa, a good friend like Constanta, and even Samuel. I am a little fearful, but Mama says that God would not have brought us this far if He did not intend to help us. Mama has known God longer than I, and I suspect she is right.

Day 66: Today we came to a harbor where the sailors let down the anchor. All the men have had a meeting and signed a paper called the Mayflower Compact. John Carver was elected our governor. Papa says it is very important to have order and laws so that everyone is accountable. He says this is a historic time and that we are carving out a new life together. I am sure Papa is a wise man, but I am more interested in having a warm house and a bed that is dry and does not roll about.

Day 67: It is our first Sunday in the New World. Today we had services of Thanksgiving on the deck with singing of Psalms, preaching, prayers, and meditation. Elder Brewster said that we shall all be sustained by the Spirit of God and His grace. It is a mighty thing to know that God is here with us. Tomorrow, the women and girls will be allowed to go ashore to wash clothes. I am looking forward to setting my feet on solid ground again. I do not mind the work at all! One day, I shall tell my children of this great voyage and how it was a time of fear and excitement, sorrow and joy, and great difficulties. But I shall also tell them that if God is with you, anything can be accomplished.

Pamela Kennedy is a freelance writer of short stories, articles, essays, and children's books. Married to a naval officer and mother of three children, she has made her home on both U.S. coasts and in Hawaii and currently resides in Washington, D.C. She draws her material from her own experiences and memories, adding bits of imagination to create a story or mood.

MASSASOIT OF THE WAMPANOAGS
Plymouth, Massachusetts
Clyde H. Smith
FPG International

To Plymouth—
with Thanks

George Sharp

Long ago, in sixteen twenty,
Came the Pilgrims seeking plenty,
Driven from their homes in England,
Driven from their haven, Holland.
Seeking freedom in their worship,
Seeking homes to live at peace in,
Through the stormy, threatening ocean,
On they came without a notion
Of that "Stern and rock-bound coast."

Cold and bitter was the weather;
Still they were all there together.
Building shelter was a struggle;
Finding food, another struggle;
Still they worked while singing praises,
Still they built with faith unshaken.
Theirs the land to pioneer in,
Not a land to faint or fear in.
Who could guess what was in store?

MAYFLOWER II
Plymouth, Massachusetts
Dick Dietrich Photography

Winter swept around their houses;
Sickness shrank their little number,
Weak was man and beast with hunger.
Still their faith was never shaken,
Still their hopes would rise, awaken
As each day would dawn anew.
Captain Standish found, exploring,
Food the Indians had been storing;
Found it when there was no other:
Corn to feed the famished brother.
Though it was so very little,
Still they shared it, ever thankful:
On each plate five grains of corn.

When in springtime crops were planted;
When their wish for peace was granted;
When the autumn brought the harvest,

Harvest that was rich and fruitful,
Pilgrims making friends with natives,
Showed their friends that they were thankful:
Thankful for their land and living.
Still, the symbol of Thanksgiving
Was for each five grains of corn.

Now as centuries pass, we're thankful,
Thankful for all God's creation.
Thankful for each gift and blessing;
Thankful for our own free nation.
Now we praise our Pilgrim fathers
For their faith in time of hardship,
Faith that makes our life worth living.
Still, the symbol of Thanksgiving
Is, for me, five grains of corn.

Nancy J. Skarmeas

Sacajawea

Popular legend claims that as Meriwether Lewis and William Clark made their way through the wilderness of the American Northwest in 1804, they found themselves in need of a guide and turned to a young Shoshoni woman known as Sacajawea. Not yet twenty years old and nursing an infant son, the legend continues, Sacajawea courageously led the Lewis and Clark expedition across the rugged and dangerous terrain of the Continental Divide, an

achievement unheard of for a woman of her time. Impressive and captivating as it is, however, the legend of Sacajawea is also partly fictitious, a simplified and idealized version of a truly tragic and inspirational life story.

Sacajawea was born in 1786 into the Lemhi band of the Shoshoni tribe. Her people lived along the Salmon River in what is now central Idaho. Little is known of her childhood until the age of fourteen, when she was taken prisoner by a war party of the Hidatsa tribe. The Hidatsa sold Sacajawea as a slave. After subsequent sales, in 1804 she became the property of Toussaint Charbonneau, a French Canadian trapper who lived among the Hidatsa.

With Charbonneau, Sacajawea found some relief from the harsh life of a prisoner and slave. She and the trapper married and together had a son, Jean Baptiste Charbonneau. Still, at the age of eighteen, Sacajawea remained a captive, separated from her home and family with no power to control the course of her own life. Her life appeared to take a turn for the worse later in 1804, when Charbonneau signed on as an interpreter for Meriwether Lewis and William Clark, two explorers leading an expedition into the wilderness to the northwest. Sacajawea and her infant son had no choice but to go along.

The legend of Sacajawea tells us that she was Lewis and Clark's principal guide; in truth, she began as nothing more than the interpreter's wife, a scared young woman traveling with an infant among a group of strange white men. As the days of the expedition wore on, however, Sacajawea took on a unique role. At first, her mere presence proved useful. The many bands of Native Americans that Lewis and Clark met in their travels were generally put at ease by the sight of a woman and an infant in the party. Occasionally, Charbonneau's knowledge of the local language was lacking, and he turned to his young wife for help; eventually she became the lead interpreter, easing communication with each tribe through whose territory the group passed. Her assistance became an everyday necessity. Sacajawea was a young, inexperienced woman, but she knew which plants were edible and how to prepare them. In her childhood, she had come to know the natural world in a way the men from the East did not, and her insight and knowledge became indispensable.

Sacajawea was already an integral part of the Lewis and Clark team when they came upon a group of natives with whom she was intimately familiar: her native Lemhi Shoshoni. In the years since Sacajawea's kidnapping, her brother had become chief of their people. The presence of his long-lost sister among these white men eased the chief's fears and suspicions, and he provided them the horses, supplies, and guides without which they would never have made it across the Continental Divide. In the end, Sacajawea's greatest contribution to Lewis and Clark was her service as a bridge between her people and the white men.

Sacajawea was not, after all, a savvy and courageous lead guide. She was, rather, a brave young woman who adapted to a new and terrifying experience and made a contribution to a great American achievement. After the Lewis and Clark expeditions, Sacajawea and her husband Charbonneau tried briefly to settle in St. Louis, but both missed life in the wilderness; they soon left the city to settle in what would become South Dakota.

According to most reports, Sacajawea died in 1812 at the age of twenty-six. Her life was in many ways a great tragedy. Taken by force as a child from her home and family, she never returned to her native way of life. The true story of Sacajawea is also inspirational, more so than the idealized legend, for the young Shoshoni woman was brave and strong; in the face of circumstances that would have defeated many, she persevered and left her mark on the history of her native land.

Tim Hamling

TAOS PUEBLO, NEW MEXICO
Bob Clemenz Photography

Taos Pueblo

In 1540, Hernando de Alvarado led a detachment of Francisco Coronado's men northward up the Rio Grande River. In search of the famed lost cities of gold, the men found something entirely different: the settlement of Taos Pueblo. One of Coronado's men recorded what they saw: "The houses are very close together, and have five or six stories, three of them mud walls and two or three with thin wooden walls, which become smaller as they go up, and each one has its own little balcony outside of the mud walls, one above the other, all around, of wood." Although over four centuries have passed since the first Europeans discovered Taos Pueblo, this description remains accurate today.

Taos Pueblo is both a village and a structure. Its land consists of 95,000 acres just north of Taos, New Mexico, in the north-central part of the state. Ruins in the Taos Valley indicate the Taos Indians have inhabited this area for nearly one thousand years. For the last six hundred years, the Indians have lived in a communal house—also called Taos Pueblo—which is divided by the Rio Pueblo de Taos River into two distinct buildings: *Hlauuma* (North House) and *Hlaukwima* (South House). The five-story pueblo consists of many individual homes, built side by side and in layers, sharing common walls but no connecting doorways. Currently, about one hundred and fifty Taos Indians live year round within Taos Pueblo. *Hlauuma* and *Hlaukwima* are considered to be the oldest continuously inhabited communities in the country.

The entire Taos Pueblo structure is made from adobe—a mixture of earth, water, and straw—which is poured into forms or formed by hand into sun-dried bricks. Wooden timbers called *vigas* (these can be seen protruding from the pueblo's walls) support the roofs. Walls are often several feet thick to support the terraced structure of the multi-storied pueblo. Each higher story sits about fifteen feet back from the one below. This space provides the upper-level homes ample work space for household chores.

The preservation of Taos Pueblo can partly be attributed to the meticulous care shown for the structure. The occupants maintain the outer walls by replastering them with thin layers of mud; interior walls are covered with thin washes of white earth, which keeps the inside walls clean and brightens each individual home. Very few windows and doors exist to let in outside light, and electricity is not allowed in the Pueblo; consequently, the white-washed walls help illuminate each home.

In addition to no electricity, Taos Pueblo prohibits running water within its walls. Rather than embrace these modern conveniences, today's Taos Indians have chosen to uphold their rich heritage. Their agrarian lifestyle enables them to produce the majority of the food they need. Skillful artisans produce clothing and other household necessities. Trading with other Pueblo Indians in the area enables the Taos Indians to acquire what they cannot produce themselves. Preserving its rich and unique cultural heritage is of primary importance to Taos Pueblo.

Perhaps the most dramatic event in the preservation of Taos Pueblo's culture and heritage occurred in 1970. In that year, the federal government returned 48,000 acres of mountain land, including the sacred Blue Lake, which they had held since 1906. For one thousand years, Blue Lake has been the focal point of the Taos Indians' cultural identity and the site of their religious ceremonies. The return of Blue Lake attests to the Taos Indians' determination to preserve their culture and heritage.

Although Blue Lake and its surrounding mountains are now off limits to outsiders, most of Taos Pueblo is open to visitors. Annual ceremonies and seasonal dances are open to the public. Some individual rooms in the Pueblo are open as curio shops offering local arts and crafts. Mica-flecked pottery and silver jewelry are two traditional crafts. The Taos Indians also work with animal skins to produce moccasins, boots, and drums.

In 1975, Taos Pueblo was declared a National Historic Landmark, and in 1987, it was nominated to the World Heritage Society as one of the most significant historical and cultural landmarks in the world. By overcoming four hundred years of external pressures, Taos Pueblo's architecture, ceremonies, and customs have proven their ability to endure amid a changing world.

Pilgrim Thanksgiving

Minnie Klemme

Prudence and Priscilla, set the festive board;
Patience, shine the pewterware;
Constance, give the word
That will bid all thankful folk
To our golden hoard.

Hester, bring the turkey, Heather, cut the pies;
Hannah, watch the pudding—
Lest, before our eyes,
Something may become amiss
That will bring us sighs.

Father, ask the blessing; each one, bow the head
That we may thank Providence
For our daily bread,
For the watch-care over us
When our way was dread . . .
Hannah, the pudding!

D. Fran Morley

Storyteller Dolls

The Storyteller Dolls of northwestern New Mexico appear ageless. It is easy to imagine them as part of a Native American tradition dating back hundreds, even thousands, of years; yet these clever and unusual dolls—seated male or female figures, usually human but sometimes animal, covered with tiny, attentive children—can be traced back to the imagination and innovative design of one person.

Helen Cordero, a potter of the Cochiti Pueblo in New Mexico, is responsible for Storyteller Dolls and is, in fact, responsible for the rebirth of artistic pottery figure making among the Native Americans of New Mexico. Before she produced her first Storyteller, Cordero was making other ordinary pottery items; she wasn't happy with her work on bowls and other containers and decided to try making pottery figures. Around 1960, she produced, among other designs, a figure of a seated woman holding a small child; the

woman's mouth is open as though she is singing. Cordero called the figure a "Singing Mother," a name and design common to Pueblo culture and, in fact, a variation on mother and child figures seen in various cultures around the world dating back to prehistoric times.

There is archeological evidence that Native Americans in the Southwest produced pottery jugs, bowls, and other containers as early as 300 B.C. Over the centuries, artists became quite adept at making pottery figures of people and animals, but when the Spanish missionaries arrived in the sixteenth century, they denounced the figures as idols. The practice of making pottery figures quickly died out and was not revived for another three hundred years.

Just as the outside influence of the Spanish priests ended figurative pottery making in the sixteenth century, another outside influence restarted it. In the 1880s, train loads of tourists eager to

L-R STORYTELLER by Alma Concha, Jemez/Taos Pueblos, NM, 1977; STORYTELLER by Juanita Arquero, Cochiti Pueblo, NM, c.1973; STORYTELLER by Serefina Ortiz, Cochiti Pueblo, NM, c. 1973; Museum of International Folk Art, a unit of the Museum of New Mexico. Photo by Blair Clark.

purchase a piece of authentic "Indian art" began arriving in the Southwest. The natives found that small, decorative figures—both traditional and brightly painted, new designs—sold well. They produced these in great numbers, and, as is often the case, quality did not improve with quantity. Through the 1950s, scholars and art collectors dismissed these figures as "toys" and discouraged their production.

When Helen Cordero began producing her pottery figures in the 1960s, the higher quality of her work attracted the attention of folk art collector Alexander Girard. Girard gave Cordero the economic freedom to experiment with her designs when he bought several of her pieces and commissioned more. Shortly thereafter, he asked if she could make a larger figure with children. In creating this design, Cordero thought about her grandfather, who was a respected Pueblo storyteller, and how he was always surrounded by his many grandchildren. She decided to make a piece in his memory. Although similar to the traditional "Singing Mother" design, Cordero's new design, which she called a "Storyteller" in honor of her grandfather, had significant variations: Cordero's first "Storyteller" is male instead of female, and it has an unrealistic placement of children.

Cordero's Storyteller Dolls were immediately successful. Her designs won awards at fairs and shows throughout the Southwest and eventually around the country; her work was exhibited in museums and featured in national magazines. Soon thereafter, other artists began producing their versions of Storytellers, but it was the initial popularity of Helen Cordero's dolls that really revived the tradition of figurative pottery in the Pueblo culture of the Southwest and made it into the respected art form it is today.

Today there are many potters producing the popular Storyteller Dolls, and the variations are endless. There are male and female Storytellers, animal and human, seated, standing, and kneeling. The number of children attached to or surrounding the Storyteller ranges from two or three to thirty or more. Some are comical, fanciful designs; others are almost reverent. There are variations common to the different families of potters, but the colors and designs of the Storytellers also vary from village to village. For example, Cochiti pottery designs traditionally feature black and terra cotta designs on a cream-colored figure, Acoma pottery is distinguished by fine, black designs on white figures, and pottery from Jemez is often tan or light brown with black and terra cotta designs.

While the Storyteller Dolls of Helen Cordero and some of the other artists are considered museum pieces and are understandably very expensive, good quality, less expensive dolls can be found at shops throughout the Southwest. The north-central part of New Mexico, around Albuquerque and Santa Fe, is considered the "home" of Storyteller Dolls. Many artists live in the pueblos at Santo Domingo, Jemez, Acoma, Zuni, and of course, Cochiti, where Helen Cordero produced her first works of art. Today the Storyteller Dolls are culturally and economically important to the Southwest and are widely seen throughout the area. It is important to remember, however, that the entire family of Storytellers can be traced back to just one person who combined old traditions, fond memories of her grandfather, and an innovative idea to develop a new tradition all her own.

STORYTELLER by Helen Cordero, Cochiti Pueblo, NM, 1964
Girard Foundation Collection in the Museum of International Folk Art,
a unit of the Museum of New Mexico. Photo by Michael Monteaux.

Archive Photos

Philadelphia Sounds "V" on Liberty Bell
Amid Patriotic and Religious Observances

This cradle of American freedom celebrated Thanksgiving today with the sounding of the code signal for victory on the Liberty Bell. War plants continued to forge their products of war and their workers partook of Thanksgiving dinners from lunch boxes.

Thousands of persons lined mid-city streets for the three-and-a-half-mile-long annual Toy-

land parade, heralding the approach of the Yuletide season, while churches conducted special services of prayer in response to President Roosevelt's proclamation that the day be one of prayer.

The Liberty Bell was sounded during a five-minute ceremony at Independence Hall, which was carried to the country on a radio network. The victory signal, three dots and a dash, was tapped out with a rubber mallet by Harper M. Tobin, past Pennsylvania commander of the Veterans of Foreign Wars.

As the muted tones died away, William H. Bechtel Jr., Philadelphia County V.F.W. commander told the nation:

"The Liberty Bell voices a nation's gratitude for freedom and a people's pledge to remember that this freedom is theirs to cherish, theirs to protect, and theirs to preserve for generations yet to come as it was preserved for us today."

A rally in Convention Hall, sponsored by the International Churchmen's committee, marked the beginning of a layman's evangelist movement throughout the country.

American servicemen on Thanksgiving furlough spent the day with their families, while soldiers and sailors of Allied nations were guests at holiday feasts arranged by civic and service organizations. Mobile canteens carried turkey and trimmings to hundreds of soldiers and civilian volunteers on duty at posts in the metropolitan area.

Members of the light cruiser *Boise*, in from the battle of the Solomons, were guests at the University of Pennsylvania-Cornell football game and later were feted by a downtown hotel.

THIS IS THANKSGIVING

Richie Tankersley

Families close-gathered
With love-gentled faces,
Memories of friendships
And warm, special places,
Heads bowed in prayer
With hand touching hand,
The smile-to-smile message
Each heart understands . . .

This is togetherness,
Sharing and living—
This is true happiness . . .
This is Thanksgiving.

Photo Opposite
FRONT DOOR IN FALL
Hebron, New Hampshire
William Johnson
Johnson's Photography

Blessings

Virginia Katherine Oliver

Thanksgiving is turkey with all the trimmings
And eating all we are able,
Gathered together with bounteous plenty
About the family table.

Thanksgiving is turning our faces homeward
To join with fathers and mothers;
Thanksgiving is caring, and it is sharing
By spreading our joy to others.

Thanksgiving is time for bowing our heads
And lifting our hearts with love
In gratitude and humility too
For our blessings from above.

Gratitude

Elisabeth Weaver Winstead

When the frost has spread a silver shawl,
And the leaves have turned to gold,
When the fields of fruitful harvest
Are a glory to behold—

When dear friends and kinfolk gather
For the feasting and the fun,
And the cheer of home and hearth fire
Fills the hearts of everyone—

Then it's time to count our blessings
For the wondrous gifts we share,
Reflected in each joyous heart
With grateful praise and prayer.

A Thanksgiving Fable

Oliver Herford

It was a hungry pussy cat
  upon Thanksgiving morn,
And she watched a thankful little mouse
  that ate an ear of corn.

"If I ate that thankful little mouse
  how thankful he should be,
When he has made a meal himself,
  to make a meal for me!

"Then with his thanks for having fed
  and his thanks for feeding me,
With all his thankfulness inside,
  how thankful I shall be!"

Thus mused the hungry pussy cat
  upon Thanksgiving Day;
But the little mouse had overheard
  and declined (with thanks) to stay.

A SLICE OF LIFE

— Edgar A. Guest —

Autumn Evenings

Apples on the table
   an' the grate-fire blazin' high,
Oh, I'm sure the whole world hasn't
   any happier man than I;
The Mother sittin' mendin'
   little stockin's toe and knee,
An' tellin' all that happened
   through the busy day to me:

John
Slobodnik

Oh, I don' know how to say it,
  but these cosy autumn nights
Seem to glow with true contentment
  an' a thousand real delights.

The dog sprawled out before me
  knows that huntin' days are here,
'Cause he dreams and seems to whimper
  that a flock o' quail are near;
An' the children playin' checkers
  till it's time to go to bed,
Callin' me to settle questions
  whether black is beatin' red;
Oh, these nights are filled with gladness,
  an' I puff my pipe an' smile,
An' tell myself the struggle an' the work
  are both worth while.

The flames are full o' pictures
  that keep dancin' to an' fro,
Bringin' back the scenes o' gladness
  o' the happy long ago,

An' the whole wide world is silent
  an' I tell myself just this—
That within these walls I cherish,
  there is all my world there is!
Can I keep the love abiding
  in these hearts so close to me,
An' the laughter of these evenings,
  I shall gain life's victory.

Edgar A. Guest began his illustrious career in 1895 at the age of fourteen when his work first appeared in the Detroit Free Press. *His column was syndicated in over 300 newspapers, and he became known as "The Poet of the People."*

Cheddar and Chive Spoonbread

1 cup water
1/4 cup enriched white hominy
    quick grits
1/4 teaspoon salt (optional)
2 tablespoons freeze-dried chives or
    1/4 cup fresh, snipped chives
3 eggs, separated
1/2 cup shredded Cheddar cheese

Heat oven to 350°. In heavy, large saucepan, bring water to a boil. Slowly stir in grits and salt, if desired. Return to a boil; reduce heat. Simmer, uncovered for 2½ to 5 minutes, stirring occasionally. Remove from heat; stir in chives. In a small bowl, beat egg yolks until thick and lemon colored. Stir egg yolks and cheese into grits mixture. In a separate bowl, beat egg whites until stiff peaks form. Carefully fold egg whites into grits and cheese mixture. Pour into a 1-quart casserole or a 5-cup soufflé dish. Bake 45 to 50 minutes or until puffed and golden brown. Serve immediately. Makes 4 servings.

Photo and recipe courtesy
The Quaker Oats Company

Thankful for What

Edna Jaques

Not for the mighty world, O Lord, tonight,
    Nations and kingdoms in their fearful might,
Let me be glad the kettle gently sings,
    Let us be thankful just for little things.

Thankful for simple food and supper spread,
    Thankful for shelter and a warm, clean bed,
For little joyful feet that gladly run
    To welcome me when all my work is done.

Thankful for friends who share my joy and mirth,
    Glad for the warm, sweet fragrance of the earth,
For golden pools of sunshine on the floor,
    For love that sheds its peace about my door.

For little friendly days that slip away,
    With only meals and bed and work and play,
A rocking chair and kindly firelight,
    For little things, let me be glad tonight.

God Is Good

Clarence Edwin Flynn

Smiling sky and reaching field
Golden with the harvest's yield,
Flowering garden, flaming wood,
All proclaim that God is good.

Cheerful hearth fire gleaming bright,
Happy faces in its light,
Love serene and understood,
Tell the story, God is good.

Words that friendly thoughts impart,
Ties that bind us, heart to heart,
Joy of human brotherhood,
Spread the news that God is good.

Roads that brighten in the sun,
Happy journeys to be run,
Little things whose truth has stood,
This their message: God is good.

CRAFTWORKS

HOT-DISH CARRIER

Mary Skarmeas

Materials:

- ½ yard reversible pre-quilted fabric
- 1½ yards piping
- 1 yard ¾-inch wide eyelet lace
- 1 yard ¼-inch wide ribbon
- 1 package double-fold bias tape
- 1 yard ⅛-inch wide cord
- 2 ½-inch wide beads
- Thread to match

Directions:

Cut two 14-inch circles from the quilted fabric; set one aside. Fold other circle into quarters to match pattern. Following pattern, measure 3½ inches along each straight edge and mark. Draw a curved line between marks. Cut along line; remove smaller circle and set aside. Cut along top of remaining folded piece to make two C-shaped pieces. Set aside.

From remaining fabric, cut two 3½- by 14½-inch strips for the handles. Fold one of the strips lengthwise with right sides together and stitch ¼ inch from the raw edge. Turn right side out and press open seam down center of strip. Cut a 14½-inch length of ribbon and eyelet. Thread ribbon through eyelet; pin to handles along seam and slip-stitch in place. Repeat steps to make second handle. Set handles aside.

To make the top of the carrier, stitch bias tape to cover the straight edges of the two C-shaped pieces, leaving ends unfinished. On the curved sides, stitch the bias tape to cover, allowing room for the cord to be threaded later. Turn the ends to the inside and stitch for a smooth finish. Set top pieces aside.

To make the padded bottom, stitch double-fold bias tape around the edge of the 7-inch circle. With wrong sides together, pin to center of large circle. Stitch in place through all layers along outer and inner edges of bias tape.

On right side of bottom piece, pin piping ¼ inch from the raw edge. Baste in place. With right sides together, pin handles in place as indicated on pattern. Stitch in place and trim edges even.

With right sides together, pin top C-shaped pieces to bottom and baste in place. Stitch through all layers ½ inch from the edge, and turn right side out.

Thread cord through bias tape around center of carrier, leaving 4 inches at each end. Slip beads on ends of cord and knot above and below beads to secure.

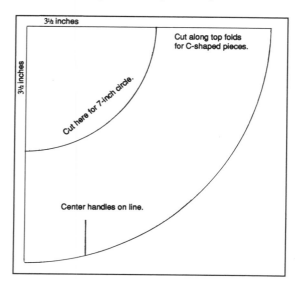

3½ inches

3½ inches

Cut along top folds for C-shaped pieces.

Cut here for 7-inch circle.

Center handles on line.

> **NOTE: Pattern is not drawn to size. Follow pattern for placement only. Follow directions for cutting.**

Photo Opposite
Gerald Koser, Photographer

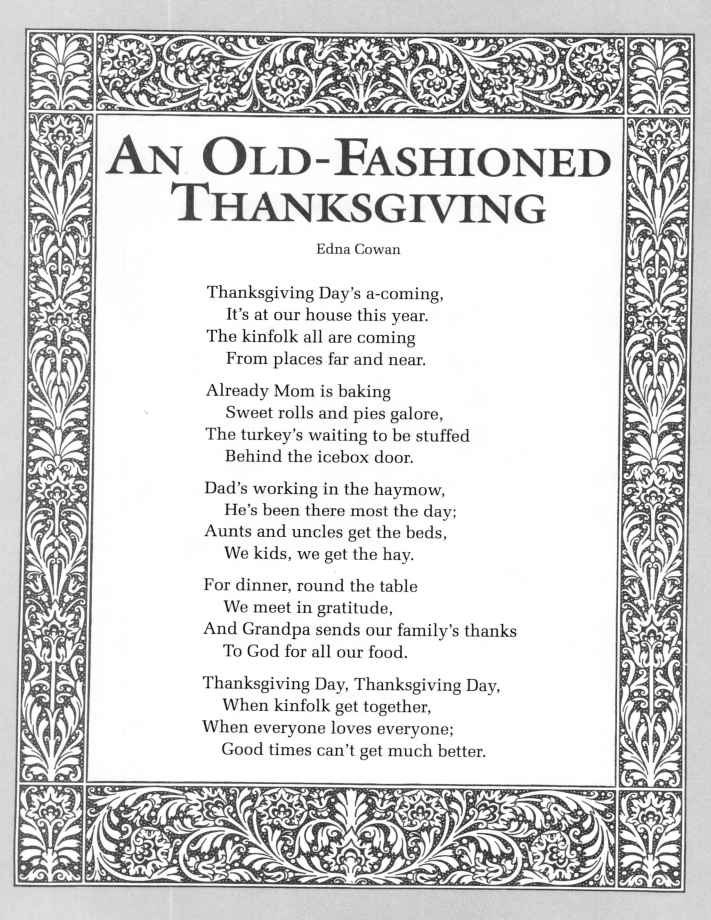

An Old-Fashioned Thanksgiving

Edna Cowan

Thanksgiving Day's a-coming,
    It's at our house this year.
The kinfolk all are coming
    From places far and near.

Already Mom is baking
    Sweet rolls and pies galore,
The turkey's waiting to be stuffed
    Behind the icebox door.

Dad's working in the haymow,
    He's been there most the day;
Aunts and uncles get the beds,
    We kids, we get the hay.

For dinner, round the table
    We meet in gratitude,
And Grandpa sends our family's thanks
    To God for all our food.

Thanksgiving Day, Thanksgiving Day,
    When kinfolk get together,
When everyone loves everyone;
    Good times can't get much better.

OUR FIRST THANKSGIVING

Donald LaVerne Walker

Come now, Martha, quit your frettin'.
   Things are looking pretty neat.
Sure a lot of fancy fussin' makes
   Thanksgiving Day complete;

But the bird is in the oven and
   There's gold upon the bun,
And that modernistic gadget
   Turns things off when they are done.

So come over, Martha darlin',
   Sit beside me while we wait
For our Johnnie and his family
   To drive through the garden gate.

Lay your head upon my shoulder,
   Let me whisper in your ear;
Let's relive the first Thanksgiving
   That we shared together, dear.

Then your silver hair was golden,
   Your eyes sparkled like the dew;
Though lines now replace your dimples,
   Yet I'm still in love with you.

Thanksgiving Day

Kay Hoffman

When the turkey's roasting brown
   And the pies are cooling near,
When your taste buds are a-tingling,
   Then Thanksgiving Day is here.

Soon the doorbell will be chiming
   With a gladsome welcome sound;
All the kinfolk will be coming
   From the many miles around.

Who cares if leaves have tumbled down
   And skies are dark and gray;
The warm, bright smile on each dear face
   Will brighten up the day.

As heads are bowed and thanks are sent
   In humble table prayer,
Each one counts his daily blessings
   Of full and ample share.

Now is the time for catching up
   On events both old and new;
What's happening in the old hometown?
   How are John and Jim and Sue?

Oh, the sound of happy voices
   To my heart will ever cling;
When the kinfolk join in song,
   How they make the rafters ring!

There's a sprinkling of snowflakes,
   And the moon is riding high;
Our goodbyes are long and heartfelt,
   A tear in many an eye.

A prayer is breathed for each loved one
   While on the homeward way:
"Take care of these dear kinfolk, Lord,
   Till next Thanksgiving Day."

A Family Grace—Thanksgiving Dinner

Peter Marshall

Father, we around this table thank Thee:
for Thy great gift of life,
that Thy love for us is not dependent
upon any worthiness of ours,
for good health,
that we know neither hunger nor want,
for warm clothes to wear,
for those who love us best,
for friends whose words of encouragement
have often chased away dark clouds,
for the zest of living,
for many an unanswered prayer,
for kindly providences that have preserved us
from danger and harm.

We thank Thee that still we live in a land
bountifully able to supply all our needs,
a land which still by Thy Providence knows
peace, whose skies are not darkened by the
machines of the enemy,
a land with peaceful valleys
and smiling meadows still serene.

O help us to appreciate all that we have,
to be content with it, to be grateful for it,
to be proud of it—not in an arrogant pride
that boasts, but in a grateful pride
that strives to be more worthy.
In Thy name, to whose bounty we owe
these blessings spread before us,
to Thee we give our gratitude.

Amen

Readers' Forum

Hannah Timmerman, Highlands, North Carolina

When we first saw this photograph of our grand-daughter, Hannah, we thought of . . . Ideals

We appreciate Ideals in many ways. It is such a wholesome magazine and has many features that honor the Lord.

Mrs. D. Ramon Walters
Augusta, Georgia

Long time *Ideals* Contributing Editor, Lansing Christman

I thought you might like to have this recent [photo] that was in our paper.

Let me take this time to say that Ideals has been my favorite publication since I was a little girl. My grandmother always kept them on her coffee table for all of us to enjoy and some forty years later they have a place on my coffee table. Never did I think that in later years, I would become very dear friends with one of your contributing editors. Lansing has been my mentor and has taught me lots about life, writing, nature, friendship, and the newspaper business. I am truly grateful that our paths have crossed because he has encouraged me immensely.

Hilda H. Morrow
Managing Editor, Inman Times
Inman, South Carolina